The Wonder Child

EMMET FOX

DeVorss & Co. Publishers
P.O. Box 550
Marina Del Rey, CA 90294-0550

No. 4

Printed in the United States of America

The Wonder Child

STRANGE as it may seem to you, there exists a mystic power that is able to transform your life so thoroughly, so radically, so completely, that when the process is completed your own friends would hardly recognize you, and in fact you would scarcely be able to recognize yourself. You would sit down and ask yourself: "Can I really be the man or woman that I vaguely remember, who went about under my name six months or six years ago? Was I really that person? Could that person possibly have been I?" And the truth will be that while in one sense you are indeed the same person, yet in another sense you will be someone utterly different. This mystic but intensely real force can pick you up today, *now*, from the midst of failure, ruin, misery, despair—and in the twinkling of an eye, as St. Paul said, solve

3

your problems, smooth out your difficulties, cut you free from any entanglements, and place you clear, safe, and happy upon the highroad of freedom and opportunity.

It can lift you out of an invalid's bed, make you sound and well once more, and free to go out into the world to shape your life as you will. It can throw open the prison door and liberate the captive. It has a magical healing balm for the bruised or broken heart.

This mystic Power can teach you all things that you need to know, if only you are receptive and teachable. It can inspire you with new thoughts and ideas, so that your work may be truly original. It can impart new and wonderful kinds of knowledge as soon as you really want such knowledge—glorious knowledge—strange things not taught in schools or written in books. It can do for you that which is probably the most important thing of all in your present stage: it can find your true place in life for you, and put you into it too. It can find the right friends for you, kindred spirits who are interested in the same ideas and want the same things that you do. It can provide you with an ideal home. It can furnish you with the prosperity that means freedom, freedom to be and to do and to go as your soul calls.

This extraordinary Power, mystic though I have rightly called it, is nevertheless very real, no mere imaginary abstraction, but actually the most practical thing there is. The existence of this Power is already well known to thousands of people in the world today, and has been known to certain enlightened souls for tens of thousands of years. This Power is really no less than the primal Power of Being, and to discover that Power is the divine birthright of all men. It is your right and your privilege to make your contact with this Power, and to allow it to work through your body, mind, and estate, so that you need no longer grovel upon the ground amid limitations and difficulties, but can soar up on wings like an eagle to the realm of dominion and joy.

But where, it will naturally be asked, is this wonderful, Mystic Power to be contacted? Where may we find it? and how is it brought into action? The answer is perfectly simple—This Power is to be found within your own consciousness, the last place that most people would look for it. Right within your own mentality there lies a source of energy stronger than electricity, more potent than high explosive; unlimited and inexhaustible. You only need to make conscious contact with this Power to set it working in your affairs; and all the marvelous results enumerated can be yours. This is the real meaning of such sayings in the Bible as "The Kingdom of God is within you"; and "Seek ye first the Kingdom of God, and all the rest shall be added."

This Indwelling Power, the Inner Light,

or Spiritual Idea, is spoken of in the Bible as a child, and throughout the scriptures the child symbolically always stands for this. Bible symbolism has its own beautiful logic, and just as the soul is always spoken of as a woman, so this, the Spiritual Idea that is born to the soul, is described as a child. The conscious discovery by you that you have this Power within you, and your determination to make use of it, is the birth of the child. And it is easy to see how very apt the symbol is, for the infant that is born in consciousness is just such a weak, feeble entity as any new-born child, and it calls for the same careful nursing and guarding that any infant does in its earliest days. After a time, however, as the weeks go by, the child grows stronger and bigger, until a time comes when it can well take care of itself; and then it grows and grows in wisdom and stature until, no longer leaning on the mother's care, the child, now arrived at man's estate, turns the tables, and repays its debt by taking over the care of its mother. So your ability to contact the mystic Power within yourself, frail and feeble at first, will gradually develop until you find yourself permitting that Power to take your whole life into its care.

The life story of Jesus, the central figure of the Bible, perfectly dramatizes this truth. He is described as being born of a virgin, and in a poor stable, and we know how he grew up to be the Saviour of the world. Now, in Bible symbolism, the virgin soul means the soul that looks to God alone, and it is this condition of soul in which the child, or Spiritual Idea, comes to birth. It is when we have reached that stage, the stage where, either through wisdom or because of suffering, we are prepared to put God really first, that the thing happens.

The Christ Child was born in a stable, though all the world had anticipated that when He arrived it would be in a palace;

and we deeply appreciate the significance of this point as soon as the Holy Child comes to birth in our own soul, for with the natural consciousness of our own unworthiness we feel only too keenly that once more He is indeed being born in a stable. Here we have the inspired intimation that this fact will not prevent His growing up to be the saviour of our own individual world.

The Bible directly and indirectly has a good deal to say on the subject of the birth and growth of the child, and what it can mean for us. One of the most significant pronouncements on this subject is given in the Book of Isaiah, chapter 9, verses 2, 6, and 7, and it will amply repay us to consider that statement in some detail.

Isaiah says: "The people that walked in darkness have seen a great light: they that dwell in the land of the shadow of death, upon them hath the light shined." This is a marvelous description of what happens when the Spiritual Idea, the child, is born to the soul. Walking in darkness, moral or physical, dwelling in the land of the shadow of death—the death of joy, or hope, or even self-respect—describes well the condition of many people before this light shines into their weary, heartbroken lives; and the Prophet rises into a paean of exultant joy as he contemplates the deliverance wrought by the mystic Power: "For unto us a child is born, unto us a son is given: and the government shall be upon his shoulder: and his name shall be called Wonderful, Counsellor, The mighty God, The everlasting Father, The Prince of Peace."

This description begins by giving the gist of the whole matter, simply and concisely—that the government is to be upon *his* shoulder. This really covers the whole business. Correctly understood, this statement tells the entire story without need of any further comment. It means that once you have contacted the mystic Power within, and have allowed it to take over your responsibilities for you, it will direct and govern all your affairs from the greatest to the least without trouble to you. *The government shall be upon his shoulder.* You are tired, and driven, and worried, and weak, and ill, and depressed, because you have been trying to carry the government upon your own shoulder; the burden is too much for you, and you have broken down under it. Now, immediately you hand over your self-government, that is the burden of making a living, or of healing your body, or erasing your mistakes, to the Child, He, the Tireless One, the All-Powerful, the All-Wise, the All-Resourceful, assumes it with joy; and your difficulties have seen the beginning of the end.

The Prophet next goes on to speak of the "Name" of the child, and if we know something of Bible symbolism, we know that we are now going to learn something funda-

mental, for in the Bible, the *Name* of any-
thing, means the character or nature of
that thing, and so we realize that a name is
not merely an arbitrary label, but actually
a hieroglyph of the soul. We are given no
less than five names or qualities of the
child. Let us examine them and see what
they tell us. First of all, Isaiah says that the
name of the child is Wonderful, and this in
fact is the first and the outstanding quality;
this child is a Wonder Child. The word
"wonderful" used here requires to be care-
fully scrutinized. As employed in the Bible,
it implies simply and plainly a miracle;
—a miracle, just that, and nothing less, because you have to realize that the Bible
teaches the miracle from the first page to
the last. The Bible repeatedly says that
miracles can happen, and that they do
happen; and it gives detailed and circum-
stantial accounts of many specific cases.
And it says, many times, that miracles always will happen if you believe them to be

possible, and are willing to recognize the Power of God, and to call upon it.

There have been many efforts during the last two generations to divorce the Bible teaching from the belief in miracles. Attempts have been made to show that in some unexplained way the Bible can be true and useful, and yet mistaken in its teaching of the miracle; in other words, that it can in some mysterious manner be an edifying conglomeration of truth and lies. Indeed, one famous Bible critic said blandly: "Miracles do not happen"—thus dismissing the whole matter with a wave of his hand. The obvious rejoinder to this is that if it were true that miracles do not happen, the Bible would be a mere meaningless jumble of pointless fables. But they do happen, and even as Galileo terminated the other controversy by saying, "nevertheless it revolves," so when all controversy finishes, we may say of miracles "nevertheless, they happen."

Well now, just recollect the first quality that Isaiah gives for the child. It is a *wonder* child; that is to say, it is a miraculous child; it is a worker of miracles. This means that as soon as the Wonder Child is born in your consciousness, the miracle will come into your life—a real miracle, remember. This does not mean simply that you will become resigned to your present circumstances, or merely that you will then be enabled to meet the same difficulties with a higher courage or a clearer brain. It means the *miracle*. It means that the Wonder Child, not in any figurative or metaphorical sense, but plainly and literally, in the most matter-of-fact meaning of the term, will work miracles in your life. It will do these things absolutely, irrespective of what your present conditions are. It is in no way constrained or constricted by your present circumstances. The whole point is that the Wonder Child can lift you out of those very circumstances, and set you down in different circumstances. The Wonder Child is the Miracle Child.

Now let us take the second point that the Prophet gives us concerning this Wonder Child. He calls it "Counsellor," and a counsellor, you know, is one who gives advice or guidance; and so you see that once the Child has been born, you need never again lack either of these things. The Child will be your infallible counsellor. If you are worried because you do not know whether or not to take some important step, to accept or reject a business offer, to sign or not to sign an important document, to enter upon or to dissolve a partnership, to resign your position or not, to go abroad or to stay at home, to trust someone or not to trust him, to say something or to leave it unsaid, the Wonder Child will be your Counsellor, and the Wonder Child is never mistaken.

It is in the third point that the Prophet reveals to us who the Wonder Child really is. It is no less than God Himself, "The Mighty God," as Isaiah reminds us, and truly the mystic Power that transforms, and transmutes, and transfigures, is *God Himself*, always present with you, and always available, once you have understood and accepted the Spiritual Idea. And it is because He is God, that the work of the Child is independent of all conditions.

The fourth name that the Prophet attributes to the Child is that of Everlasting Father. This point establishes our relationship to God in unmistakable terms. As Jesus so clearly pointed out, God is our Father, not merely our Creator, and we as the children of a good Father may expect to find ourselves provided with everything that we need for body and soul. But since we have to establish for ourselves our own consciousness of this fact, and as our demonstration is just the measure of our understanding of it, our concept of the divine fact is the fruit of our own soul, and may mystically be called our child.

Finally, in the fifth point, we receive what is perhaps the greatest name of all. Here the Child is called "The Prince of Peace." Just try to realize a little what this title must mean for you in practice— nothing less than that the Wonder Child, the Spiritual Idea, born to your own soul, is the Prince of Peace. Now think what perfect peace of soul, if you could attain it, would actually mean to you. If your soul were truly at peace, what in your life could go wrong? If only you had real peace of soul, do you suppose that your body could be ill? Given real peace of soul, how easy it would be to find your true place in the world, which would mean prosperity as well as happiness. How easily, how quickly and efficiently you could perform your work, work such as you have never done yet, and in less than half the

usual time. Of course, everybody knows
that this is what would follow the attain-
ment of soul peace, but there is still much
more in it than that. What you perhaps do
not know is that once you have attained
true peace of soul, you have made it possible for the Mystic Power, the Wonder
Child, to teach you new things, utterly
beyond the compass of your present understanding, enabling you to do things in the
world, if you should wish to, that nobody
would have deemed it possible that you
could do. Well, it is in the very nature of
the Wonder Child to give you just that
very soul peace, and it is because of this
function that it is called "The Prince of
Peace".

Isaiah goes on to tell us that this is no
limited demonstration, but that once it begins, it goes on and on as we rise higher
and higher in consciousness, increasing
and expanding more and more unto the
perfect day. "Of the increase of his government and peace there shall be no end,

upon the throne of David, and upon his kingdom, to order it, and to establish it with judgment and with justice from henceforth even forever." The throne of David is of course Jerusalem, which is Uru-Salem, the city of peace, this very peace that we have been discussing; and Jerusalem symbolically is the awakened consciousness. There shall indeed be no end to the increase of *that* government, and in view of the possibility that the weaker souls, the fearful, and the unbelieving, and the depressed, should find it impossible to believe that such good tidings could possibly be true, the Prophet clinches the matter with the definite assertion: "The Zeal of the Lord of Hosts will perform this." This should remove all sense of personal responsibility for the demonstration, the bugbear of so many seekers. Have we not seen that the gist of the whole matter is just this very point—that the government shall be upon *his* shoulder.

THE EMMET FOX BOOKS

Emmet Fox's Golden Keys to Successful Living
Spiritual discoveries that helped millions achieve happiness; set against Emmet Fox's own life, with Reminiscences by Herman Wolhorn, friend and associate.

Power Through Constructive Thinking
27 of the above booklets and cards in one volume.

The Sermon on the Mount
This book constitutes a complete course of instruction in Scientific Christianity. This is the standard textbook. Includes the Lord's Prayer.

The Ten Commandments
Master Key to Life. A companion volume to The Sermon on the Mount.

Find and Use Your Inner Power
Messages of help and inspiration for days of discouragement.

Make Your Life Worth While
Inspirational Messages for the Christian Life.

Alter Your Life
This book contains sixteen of the latest Emmet Fox pamphlets, plus some unpublished material.

Stake Your Claim
Short, to-the-point messages.

Around the Year with Emmet Fox
Selections from the inspiring teaching of Emmet Fox attractively arranged for daily meditation.

Diagrams For Living
Simple keys to unlocking the mysteries of the Bible and at the same time giving practical answers to the challenges of modern-day living.